T0199134

GOD'S PATH
TO HEAVEN

Inspired by God
Told by Jason Hammerberg
Illustrated by Janette Hill

There is only one God and He lives in Heaven. He created the Earth and everything that lives on the Earth, simply by the power of His words.

Genesis 1:1

God is all powerful — which means He can do anything!

Exodus 20:11

He lovingly created people to enjoy the Earth and follow His plan for their lives.

Genesis 2:16-17

He didn't want to force them to follow Him, so He gave them the opportunity to make their own choices and decisions. However, they made bad choices and decisions, which God calls sin.

Romans 3:23

Arrogant **Stealing** Disrespectful LAZY diso

IDOLATOR JE

IMPATIENT TH

MEAN NASTY Murdere

God in Heaven is holy. That means He has never
sinned, and He can't have sin in His home, Heaven.
He knows sin causes sadness and hurt,
and it separates people from Him.

However, God loves us even though we are sinners, and
He wants us to live forever with Him in Heaven.

Isaiah 59:2

We try to reach to God by being as good as we can, but our efforts to earn our way to Heaven are useless. There is nothing we can do to break through the sin barrier that separates us from God.

How can we get rid of our sin so we can live with God someday in Heaven? He knew we needed a way to have our sin forgiven. So, God in Heaven created the perfect master plan to show the world His love.

Isaiah 64:6 & Romans 3:20

That plan involved Jesus, God's one and only Son, to be our Savior. Jesus miraculously arrived as a special baby in Bethlehem over two thousand years ago.

Matthew 1:21-23

God's gift to us was His sinless
Son, Jesus. He was announced by angels, and
we still celebrate his birth every Christmas.

Luke 2:7-14

Growing up as a boy in the town of Nazareth, Jesus never sinned, not even once. He started teaching others in the temple at the early age of twelve.

1 Peter 2:22

All who heard Him were greatly surprised at His knowledge about the Old Testament laws and the prophets. People listened to His teachings and they were amazed!

Luke 2:41-49

Through the next several years, Jesus grew both spiritually and physically. People were drawn to Him everywhere He went.

Luke 2:52

He was announced and baptized by His cousin, John, at the age of thirty. This is when His ministry began.

Luke 3:21-23 & John 1:29-34

Jesus chose His twelve disciples and trained them one by one.

Luke 5:1-11

He was able to do things that only God could do. This proved that He was really God's Son. His disciples began to see and experience His great power.

He used parables, simple stories, to help them understand the spiritual lessons.

The Seed Sower

The Lost Sheep

The Good Samaritan

Mark 4 & Romans 3:20-23

Jesus taught that He was the one and only way to Heaven. Some people were furious when He said He was God's Son, the promised Messiah.

John 14:6

These people plotted to destroy Jesus. They did not realize that He was part of God's master plan to save the world.

John 10:30-33

At the last supper, Jesus explained to His disciples
that soon He would not be with them anymore.
He showed them how to remember
Him when He was gone.

Luke 22

Later that evening, He prayed to His Heavenly Father in the Garden of Gethsemane.

Jesus knew that He was going to be arrested, accused of crimes that were not true and sentenced to death.

Jesus, who never sinned, was preparing to die for all the sins of everyone in the whole world — sins in their past, present, and future.

John 18:4 & Romans 5:8

God is holy and hates sin. He knows that we are sinners and that we cannot get rid of sin on our own. This is the most important reason God sent His precious Son to this Earth.

Isaiah 53:5-6 & Romans 1:18

Even though Jesus was still sinless, He died
upon a cross, paying a price we could never pay.
He saved us from the punishment that our sin deserves:
our death and separation from God in Heaven.

2 Corinthians 5:21 & John 19:30

This would
be a sad story
— if it ended here ...

Because on the third day, the good news spread that Jesus was no longer dead!

He had risen and conquered death!

Mark 16 & John 20

The story was no longer that Jesus died, but that Jesus died ...
and LIVES! We still celebrate this every Easter!

Many people saw Him again
and even touched His scars!

1 Corinthians 15:1-7

Ephesians 2:8-9

Doing good things in life is important. However, it won't get you into heaven. God doesn't look at our deeds on a scale and decide if our good outweighs our bad.

God's word, the Bible, clearly says that everyone falls short of Heaven because of their sins.

We cannot earn our way into Heaven by doing good things. It is a gift from God.

Romans 3:23 & 6:23

Jesus is now in Heaven, greeting those who enter in.
Not because of good things that they have done,
but because He forgave their sins.

So, today, the question comes to you.

Will you receive
God's perfect gift?

John 3:16-18

I_____,

Receive God's free gift of salvation
through Jesus' death on the cross.

I understand why Jesus had to come to Earth
and die for my sins. My sins separate
me from God in Heaven.

I believe that through Jesus' miraculous birth,
sinless life, undeserved death, and God-given
resurrection, I can be cleansed from all of my sin.

I know I can't earn my way into Heaven.
I don't deserve it. It is simply a gift
from my loving God.*

It is 100% Jesus and 0% me.

Signed _____   Date _____

"For by grace are you saved through faith, not of yourselves, it is a gift from God.
Not of works least any one should boast. For we are God's handiwork created in the
image of Jesus to do the good things prepared before hand for us."
Ephesians 2:8-10 (NIV)

This book is called '100% Jesus!' Do you know what that actually means? 100% means ...

All, fully, completely, and totally.

Think of it like when your battery is 100% charged. It can't possibly be any more!

Jesus gave 100% of himself on the cross when He died to forgive all of our sins: past, present and future. We can't add to what has been fully, completely and totally paid for already by Jesus — just believe and receive the gift.

What should I do now that I know I am going to Heaven?

Jesus promised to be with us in Spirit, even though he is back in Heaven with God, His Father. Read about how Jesus acted on Earth and how He treated people. Through His Spirit, He will give us the strength to accomplish His plans — let's join him!

1 Corinthians 3:14, Matthew 28:19-20 & Ephesians 2:8-10

Design what you think your mansion in Heaven would look like. What color would it be? Would it have a yard? Who would live there with you? Would you have friends and neighbors live next door? Imagine that God built you a place to live for the rest of your life. What would it look like?

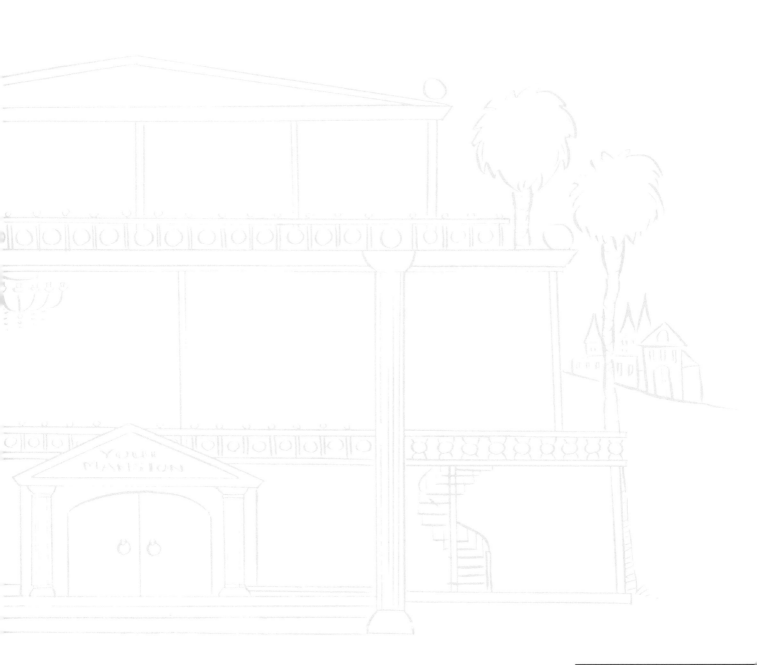

John 14:2-3

The Life of Jesus

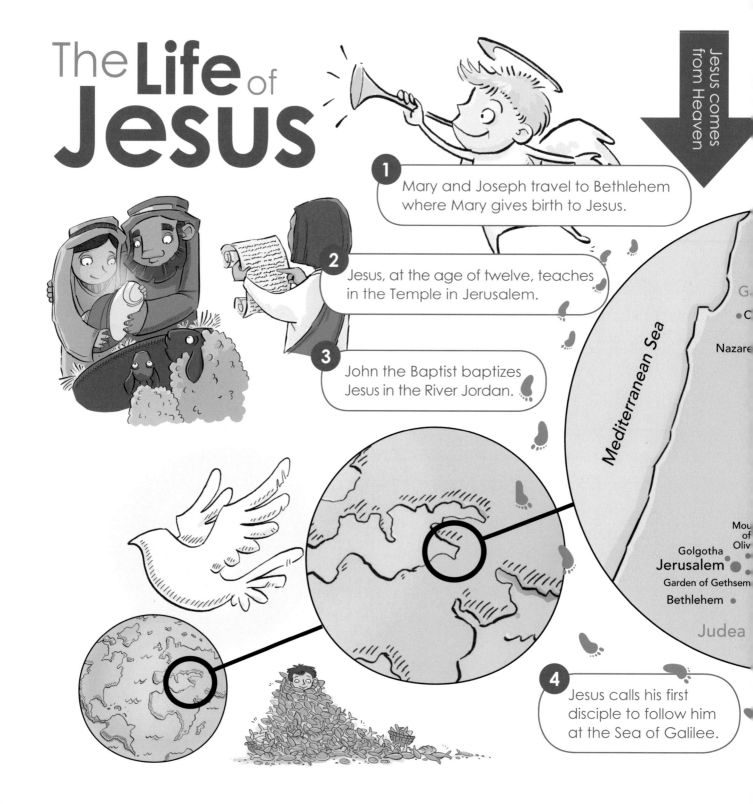

Jesus comes from Heaven

1 Mary and Joseph travel to Bethlehem where Mary gives birth to Jesus.

2 Jesus, at the age of twelve, teaches in the Temple in Jerusalem.

3 John the Baptist baptizes Jesus in the River Jordan.

4 Jesus calls his first disciple to follow him at the Sea of Galilee.

Mediterranean Sea

Nazare

Golgotha
Jerusalem
Garden of Gethsem
Bethlehem

Mou
of
Oliv

Judea

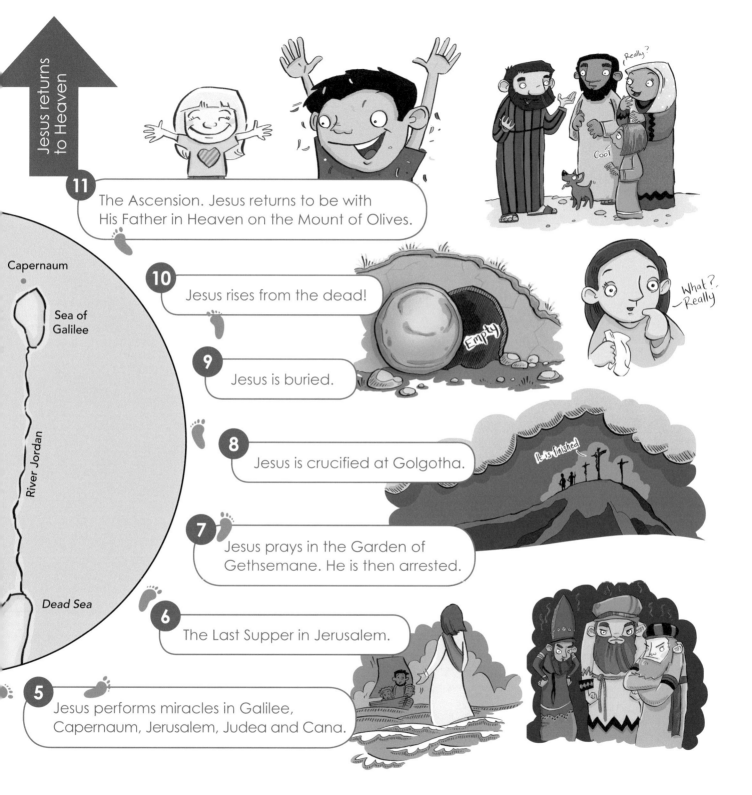

Jesus returns to Heaven

11 The Ascension. Jesus returns to be with His Father in Heaven on the Mount of Olives.

Capernaum

Sea of Galilee

River Jordan

Dead Sea

10 Jesus rises from the dead!

9 Jesus is buried.

8 Jesus is crucified at Golgotha.

7 Jesus prays in the Garden of Gethsemane. He is then arrested.

6 The Last Supper in Jerusalem.

5 Jesus performs miracles in Galilee, Capernaum, Jerusalem, Judea and Cana.

Quick Biblical Reference Guide

Look the references up in your Bible.
Read the story for yourself.

Genesis 1:1
Exodus 20:11

Genesis 2:16-17
Romans 3:23

Isaiah 59:2 & 64:6
Romans 3:20

Matthew 1:21-23

Luke 2:7-14

1 Peter 2:22

Luke 2:41-49

Luke 2:52

Luke 3:21-23
John 1:29-34

Luke 5:1-11

Matthew 14 & 15

John 3:9-10

Mark 4
Romans 3:20-23

John 14:6

John 10:30-33

Luke 22

John 18:4
Romans 5:8

Isaiah 53:5-6
Romans 1:18

2 Corinthians 5:21
John 19:30, Isaiah 53:5-6
Romans 1:18

Mark 16
John 20

1 Corinthians 15:1-7

Ephesians 2:8-9

Romans 3:23 & 6:23

John 3:16-18

Matthew 28:19-20
1 Corinthians 3:14
Ephesians 2:8-10

John 14:2-3

Jason Hammerberg

After years of teaching Sunday school, Jason could see and hear the kids' confusion about the Bible and the story of Jesus. He was inspired by this, and decided to create a kid-friendly book to teach them about the life of Jesus. The book would show them a snapshot of Jesus' time on this Earth and explain why He had to come into this world. He wanted to show them that the same baby they celebrate on Christmas is the same man they honor at Easter. The limited scripture references help the kids learn the Bible, understand that this story isn't fictional and verify the places where Jesus walked on a modern-day map. Make no mistake — this is God's story, and He inspired and directed throughout the entire process.

Philippians 4:13

Janette Hill - Illustration

Psalm 139:14

WestBow Press books may be ordered through booksellers or by contacting:

WestBow Press
A Division of Thomas Nelson & Zondervan
1663 Liberty Drive
Bloomington, IN 47403
www.westbowpress.com
844-714-3454

Because of the dynamic nature of the Internet, any web addresses or links contained in this book may have changed since publication and may no longer be valid. The views expressed in this work are solely those of the author and do not necessarily reflect the views of the publisher, and the publisher hereby disclaims any responsibility for them.

Interior Image Credit: Janette Hill

Scripture quotations are taken from The Holy Bible, New International Version®, NIV® Copyright © 1973, 1978, 1984, 2011 by Biblica, Inc.® Used by permission. All rights reserved worldwide.

ISBN: 978-1-6642-7507-2 (sc)
ISBN: 978-1-6642-7508-9 (e)

Library of Congress Control Number: 2022914634

Print information available on the last page.

WestBow Press rev. date: 08/23/2022

WESTBOW
PRESS®
A DIVISION OF THOMAS NELSON
& ZONDERVAN

Printed in the United States
by Baker & Taylor Publisher Services